100 EASY-TO-MAKE
GOAN DISHES

CW01619189

JENNIFER FERNANDES

TARANG PAPERBACKS
a division of
VIKAS PUBLISHING HOUSE PVT LTD

VIKAS PUBLISHING HOUSE PVT LTD
576, Masjid Road, Jangpura, New Delhi - 110014

COPYRIGHT © JENNIFER FERNANDES, 1977

Twenty-Second Edition, 1993

Printed Hindustan Offset Printers, Delhi-32.

Introduction

Goa. It's an experience quite unlike any other. Where slowing down the pace of life comes as naturally as sipping cashew feni, or calling on St. Anthony to hurry the monsoon along to quench a parched field; where a boisterous three-day carnival precedes the de-mothballing of black Lenten suits; where a piano is part of the furniture in most homes and violin lessons start soon after kindergarten; where friendly *tavernas* beckon thirsty travellers, and where Conception D'Albuquerque shares a beer with Visitation Alphonso and wonders what the stranger finds so amusing about their good Christian names.

History tells us that in their search for the New World, intrepid Portuguese seamen discovered India. Soon Goa had become the bastion of their Eastern Empire. As conquerors, they more than met their match in the Dutch, the French and the British. But their missionaries and their customs left a more lasting impression. Corinthian facades and baroque interiors mark the monasteries and cathedrals which, to this day, vie for pride of place with Hindu temples and Muslim mosques. Christmas is still a time for exchanging greetings and trays of home-made sweets. In fact, nowhere is the Portuguese influence so evident as in Goan food. But there too, as in all else, the all-pervading Goan colour comes through with a generous dash of red chilly here and an innovative splash of coconut milk there.

Traditional Goan cooking calls for plenty of muscle and time. Grinding is always part of the recipe and the nicer the dish the longer it takes to make. For instance, the original recipe for Bibinca starts with, 'Take 4 dozen eggs' and ends with, 'Cooking time, 10 hours.' In this book, I have tried to introdue the modern housewife to some of Goa's specialities knowing that the kitchen is not her only preoccupation.

Much of the inspiration comes from the casually narrated recipes of my grandmother, the painstaking, hand-written collection of my mother, the improvisations of an elder sister and the encouragement of a husband who served as chief guinea-pig through all my experiments. To them, and to you, dear reader, I can only say like a grateful Goan, '*Deo boren korum*',[1] a phrase that will add a touch of authenticity if used when you are seeing your guests off at the end of your first experiment with Goan cooking.

Jennifer Fernandes

[1]A traditional way of saying 'Thank you', the literal meaning being, 'May God do good things for you.'

Useful Tips

1. Goan food is pungent and I have used the required amount of chillies to keep the recipes as authentic as possible. However, if one is not accustomed to such hot food, the chillies may be cut down to suit individual tastes. In Goan cooking, Kashmiri and Goa chillies are used, which are milder than the other varieties available.

2. To extract coconut juice, cover the grated coconut with boiling water. When it cools, pass it through a blender for a couple of minutes. Then strain. This gives you a thick juice. If you need some more, repeat the process and you will get a thin juice.

3. To cook rice, the quantity of water is always double the quantity of rice, i.e., 1 cup of rice to 2 cups of water. Bring this to a boil, then cover firmly to make sure the steam does not escape and cook on a slow fire for about 12 minutes for a small quantity—up to $1\frac{1}{2}$ cups of rice.

4. Since grinding is a problem, wherever possible pass the dry ingredients (i.e. cumin, coriander, pepper, etc.) through an electric grinder. I grind coconut in large quantities, divide it into the required number of portions and keep it in individual packets in the freezer. This lasts for over 6 months. Also, the red chillies can be ground in vinegar (remove the seeds to make it milder) and stored in

a plastic container in the refrigerator. Tamarind is now available in a concentrated form, marketed under the brand name of 'Tamcon.'

To make a quick curry, then, all you do is mix the ground coconut (thawed) with a teaspoon of ground red chillies and then add the dry spices.

5. Tamarind makes meat, fish, etc., tough, so be sure to cook the meat and add the tamarind 10 minutes before removing the meat from the fire.

6. Vinegar, when cooked for a long time, tends to become bitter. Add this only at the last minute.

7. When making a fish curry, add the fish only after the massalas and water have come to a rolling boil, as the fish should not be cooked too long, or it tends to disintegrate.

8. To peel tomatoes—plunge them into boiling water, cover the pan and leave for 5 minutes. Remove each one with a fork and the skin will peel off quite easily.

9. Since almonds are expensive, substitute them with cashew-nuts. Grate the cashews in a grinder and use almond essence in the recipe. Or, after grating, grind on a stone, using rose water to make it into a paste, and then add almond essence to taste.

10. Oven temperatures:

Hot	400°—475°
Moderate	325°—375°
Slow	275°—325°

CONTENTS

SOUPS 1
FISH 9
RICE AND CURRY 29
PORK 49
CHICKEN AND MEAT 59
PICKLES AND CHUTNEYS 87
SWEETS 99
GLOSSARY 125

SOUPS

1

Meat Soup

½ kg. meat or bones
3 tomatoes
¼" piece ginger
4 flakes garlic
1 onion (chopped)
pepper and salt to taste
alphabet or any small macaroni
a few mint or celery leaves

Put all the ingredients together, except the macaroni, in a pan, and bring it to a boil. Remove the scum that forms on the top and simmer the soup on a slow fire, without a lid, for 2 hours. Strain, add the macaroni, and boil till the macaroni is tender.

Serves 6

2

Tomato Soup

1 kg. tomatoes
4 cloves
1 bay leaf
1 large onion
1 tsp. sugar
small piece cinnamon
1 large carrot (chopped)
1 tblsp. butter
1 dessertspoon flour
salt and pepper to taste

Boil the tomatoes with the cloves, bay leaf, onion, sugar, cinnamon, carrot and the seasoning till the tomatoes and carrot turn pulpy. Strain and set aside.

Melt the butter, add the flour and cook for 2 minutes. Then add the strained juice and stir till thick. If desired, serve with a swirl of cream on each serving.

Serves 6

3

Vegetable/Meat Soup

2 carrots
1 capsicum
1 large potato
1 bunch leeks or 1 onion
1 stalk celery
4 tomatoes
4 cups stock or 4 soup cubes, diluted in 4 cups water
¼ kg peas
macaroni (optional)
a little cabbage (grated)
salt and pepper to taste

Chop the vegetables and fry in a little butter or oil. Put the tomatoes through a blender, and add to the vegetables. Next, add the stock, salt and pepper and when it comes to a boil, add the peas and macaroni. Cook till the peas and macaroni are tender, then add the grated cabbage and cook for a minute. Remove from fire and serve.

Serves 6

4

Dal Soup

1½ cups dal (moong or massoor)
1 large ham bone or 3 slices bacon
2 carrots (chopped)
1 onion (chopped)
4 tomatoes (chopped and peeled)
salt and pepper to taste
bread croutons (optional)

Put the dal, bacon, chopped carrots, onion and seasoning in a pan, cover with water and cook till the dal is soft. Add the chopped, peeled tomatoes and the salt and cook again till the tomatoes are pulpy. Remove from fire, and cool. Put the soup through a blender, reheat and serve.

If using croutons, cut slices of bread into cubes and fry in oil till crisp. Drain on absorbent paper.

Serves 6

5

Prawn Soup

½ kg. medium size prawns
½ tsp. turmeric
¼" piece ginger
1 potato
2 onions (chopped)
2 tomatoes (chopped)
1 tblsp. butter
1 tsp. flour
salt and pepper to taste

Wash prawns and boil with the turmeric, ginger, potato, one onion, tomatoes and seasoning. When the prawns are cooked, remove shells and heads. Crush shells and heads and reserve the juice. Strain this juice along with the broth and set the prawns aside.

Melt the butter and fry the remaining chopped onion and the flour. Cook for 2 minutes. Pour in the broth and prawns and boil for a few minutes. Serve hot.

Serves 6

FISH

6

Prawn Baffad

¼ kg. prawns (shelled)
8 Kashmiri chillies
½ tsp. cumin
12 peppercorns
2-3 flakes garlic
½" piece ginger
1 tsp. turmeric
2 medium onions (chopped)
1 large tomato (chopped)
salt to taste
tamarind and vinegar to taste

Grind together the chillies, cumin, peppercorns, garlic and ginger and mix in the turmeric powder.

Fry the onions, and add the tomato and prawns. Fry well. Next, add the ground massalas, and the tamarind and vinegar. Cover and cook till the prawns are done.

Serves 4

7

Prawn Cutlets

¼ kg. prawns (shelled)
1 medium onion (minced)
1-2 green chillies (chopped)
1 bunch coriander leaves
2-3 flakes garlic (chopped)
small piece of ginger (chopped)
salt and pepper to taste
½ tsp. each cloves, cinnamon
and cardamom
½ tsp. turmeric powder
1 sour lime (juice)
2 eggs
1 slice of bread (soaked and drained)
breadcrumbs

Mince prawns and mix well with chopped onion, chillies, coriander, garlic and ginger. Add the lime juice, garam massala and bread. Beat eggs. Shape mixture into rounds, dip in beaten egg, then breadcrumbs, and fry.

Serves 4

8

Prawn Balchao

¼ kg. prawns (shelled)
i tsp. cumin
1 tsp. pepper
10 Kashmiri chillies
vinegar to taste
1 tsp. turmeric
2 cups oil
4 medium onions (minced)
2 large sprigs curry leaves
1" piece ginger (chopped)
3 whole pods garlic (chopped)
4-5 green chillies (seeded and chopped)
salt to taste

Grind together the cumin, pepper and Kashmiri chillies in vinegar and mix in the turmeric. Heat the oil and fry the onions. Onions should be fried till all the water is dry. Add the prawns and the ground massala. Next add the curry leaves, and the chopped ginger, green chillies and garlic. Add salt and vinegar to taste and simmer till well cooked. (This should be eaten with rice and curry.)

Serves 4

9

Prawn Chilly Fry

¼ kg. prawns (shelled)
6 onions (sliced)
2-3 green chillies (chopped)
½" piece ginger (chopped)
¼ tsp. chilly powder
½ tsp. turmeric
¼ tsp. ground pepper
salt to taste

Fry the onions till soft. Add the green chillies, ginger and powdered massalas. Lastly, add the prawns and cook till dry. (This should be eaten together with rice and curry.)

Serves 4

10

Rache Pomfret

1 large pomfret (cleaned and kept whole)
5 red Kashmiri chillies
$\frac{1}{4}$ tsp. cumin
1-2 flakes garlic
3 peppercorns
a walnut-size ball of tamarind
$\frac{1}{4}$" piece of ginger
vinegar and salt to taste

Make two slits on both sides of the pomfret and on either side of the bone. Grind together the chillies, cumin, garlic, peppercorns, tamarind and ginger in vinegar. Add salt to taste. Stuff the pomfret with the massalas, on either side of the slit. Secure the fish with a string and fry till both sides are brown. Remove the string and serve. (Mackerel may also be used instead of pomfret.)

Serves 4

11

Mackerel Salad

2-3 dried mackerel
2 green chillies (sliced)
1 large onion (minced)
vinegar and salt to taste

Grill or fry the mackerel and flake into small pieces. Mix in the chillies, onion and vinegar and salt. (This should be eaten with rice and curry.)

Serves 4

12

Parra (Salt Fish Pickle)

50 pieces of salt fish or mackerel to be washed in vinegar, sprinkled with turmeric powder and dried in the sun for a day

1½ cups cumin
½ cup peppercorns
4 whole pods of garlic
6" piece ginger
4 cups chilly powder
1½ cups turmeric

Grind the cumin, peppercorns, 2 pods of garlic and approximately half the ginger in vinegar. Mix in the chilly powder and turmeric.

Crush the remaining 2 pods of garlic and ginger. Mix this with the ground massala and the fish. Put it in an earthernware crock and cover the fish with vinegar. Pickle for about a month, at least, before using. Before serving, take out the mackerel and shallow fry quickly on both sides for a minute or two. (This is an accompaniment with rice and curry.)

13

Caldine (Yellow Fish Curry)

1 medium pomfret (prawns could also be substituted)
½ coconut (scraped)
¼ tsp. cumin
1 tsp. turmeric powder
2-3 flakes garlic
½" piece ginger
1 medium onion (chopped)
2-3 whole green chillies
tamarind and salt to taste
coriander leaves for garnishing

Soak the coconut in boiling water. When cool, pass through a blender. Strain the milk and set aside. Add more warm water, cumin, turmeric, garlic and ginger to the coconut and pass through the blender once again. Strain and set this thin juice aside.

Cut the fish into slices and fry if desired. Fry the onion. Next, add the thick and thin juices of the coconut and the green chillies, slit lengthwise. When this comes to a boil, add the fish and cook till done. Finally, add the tamarind and salt to taste. Garnish with coriander.

Serves 2-3

14

Stuffed Pomfret

1 large pomfret
½ coconut
1 large bunch coriander leaves
2 flakes garlic
¼" piece ginger
walnut-size ball of tamarind
2 green chillies
sugar and salt to taste
3 peppercorns

Chutney: scrape and grind fine the coconut together with coriander leaves, garlic, ginger, tamarind, green chillies, salt, sugar and peppercorns.

Leave the pomfret whole and slit on either side. Stuff with the chutney, secure with a string, dot with ghee and bake in a moderate oven, till done. Remove string, and serve garnished with sliced lemon.

Serves 4

15

Fried Bombay Duck (fresh)

8 fresh Bombay ducks
$\frac{1}{2}$ tsp. turmeric
salt to taste
$\frac{1}{4}$ tsp. chilly powder
1 cup flour

Remove the centre bone of the fish, flatten and keep under a weight for an hour. Squeeze out all the water.

Add the turmeric, salt and chilly powder to the flour. Dip fish in this mixture and pat on both sides. Shallow fry and serve hot. Alternatively, after squeezing out the water, sprinkle the fish with turmeric, chilly powder and salt. Dip in a beaten egg and breadcrumbs and fry.

Serves 4

16

Fried Bombay Duck (dried)

8 dried Bombay ducks
1 tsp. turmeric
¼ tsp. chilly powder
salt to taste

Soak the Bombay ducks in water and remove the central bone. Squeeze out all the water. Sprinkle turmeric, chilly powder and a little salt and fry. Alternatively, flatten the fish after squeezing out water. Stuff with rache massala, (see Recipe 10) tie with string and fry.

Serves 4

17

Fried Fish or Prawns

1 pomfret or $\frac{1}{4}$ kg. prawns
1 tsp. turmeric
$\frac{1}{2}$ tsp. chilly powder
salt to taste
juice of $\frac{1}{2}$ a lemon

Marinate the fish in the turmeric, chilly powder, salt and lemon juice for half an hour. Fry till brown, and serve hot.

Serves 2

18

Fish Rissoles

1 large or 2 medium pomfret or any fleshy fish
2 large tomatoes (chopped)
1 tsp. turmeric
½ tsp. chilly powder
½ tsp. ground pepper
½ tsp. salt
1 tblsp. butter
a bunch of coriander and mint leaves
1 large onion (minced)
1-2 green chillies (minced)
juice of one lemon
5 medium boiled and mashed potatoes
1 large egg
breadcrumbs
1 tblsp. flour

Boil the fish with the tomatoes and a little water. Mash and set aside. Mix in the turmeric, chilly powder, pepper, salt, butter, coriander and mint, onion, green chillies and lemon juice. Add the mashed potato and egg yolk. Beat the egg white a little, shape the mixture into rissoles, dip in the egg white and breadcrumbs and fry.

Serve with the sauce made up of the strained stock after boiling the fish, thickened with flour and seasoned with salt and pepper.

Serves 6

19

Baked Crab

4 medium crabs
1 onion (minced)
1 dessertspoon curry powder
1-2 green chillies (chopped)
½" piece ginger (chopped)
3-4 flakes garlic (chopped)
1 slice of bread (soaked in coconut milk)
salt to taste

Plunge the crabs in boilings, salted water. Remove the flesh from the shell, and set aside. Brown the onion in oil and add the curry powder, green chillies, ginger, garlic and bread. Add the flesh of the crabs and cook till dry. Fill back into crab shells and brown under a hot grill.

Serves 4

20

Fish and Mayonnaise Sauce

1 large pomfret (or any other fleshy fish)
2-3 tomatoes (chopped)
½" piece ginger (chopped)
3 flakes garlic (chopped)
2 tblsp. butter
1 dessertspoon flour
salt to taste
1 egg (yolk only)
mustard, chilly and pepper powders
1 cup milk
1 dessertspoon olive oil (optional)
2 tblsp. grated cheese
salad of tomatoes, onions and cucumber

Boil the fish with the tomatoes, ginger and garlic and enough water to just cover the fish.

Melt the butter and add the flour, gradually. Beat the egg yolk with the seasoning, beat in the milk and add it to the butter/flour mixture. Cook on a slow fire till thick, stirring all the time. When it cools add the olive oil and the grated cheese. Serve fish surrounded with the salad, and pour the sauce over the whole.

Serves 4

21
Fish Cachets

(This can be served either as an hors d'oeuvre or as a main dish.)

Pastry *2 cups flour*
1 cup soojee
salt to taste
1 cup butter or ghee
3 eggs
salt and pepper to taste
a little milk to bind

Filling *1 tin of any fish (salmon preferred)*
2 tblsp. oil (preferably olive)
1 dessertspoon grated cheese
2 green chillies, seeded and chopped
¼ tsp. chilly powder and mustard
pepper and salt to taste

Sauce *yolk of 1 hard-cooked egg*
a little vinegar
1 dessertspoon oil
1 tsp. sugar

For the pastry: Mix the flour, soojee and salt with the

butter till the texture resembles breadcrumbs. Add the egg (yolks only) and the milk to form a soft dough. Knead well and either form into individual cachets or line a large dish with the pastry and bake in a hot oven.

For the filling: Put the oil in a pan and when hot, add the fish, cheese, green chillies, chilly-powder seasoning and the gravy of the fish. Cook till the gravy dries. Set aside.

For the sauce: Mix the yolk of the hard-cooked egg with the vinegar to form a paste. Add seasoning, oil and sugar and mix till the sugar dissolves.

Place the fish onto the baked shell. Garnish with tomatoes and the whites of the hard-cooked egg, and spoon the sauce over.

Serves 6

butter all the [illegible] except [illegible]. Add the egg yolks [illegible] and the milk [illegible] a soft dough. Knead well [illegible] a large dish [illegible] the pastry and bake in a hot oven.

For the filling: [illegible] cheese [illegible] seasoning and [illegible]. Set aside.

[illegible] pastry [illegible] with the [illegible]. Add [illegible].

Place the dish [illegible] baked [illegible] until [illegible] golden brown.

RICE AND CURRY

22

Coconut Rice

3 cups Basmati or any fine rice
1 large, fresh coconut (grated)
3 tblsp. ghee
1 large onion (finely sliced)
½ tsp. whole peppercorns
2 tsps. turmeric
1 tsp. salt

Grate the coconut, soak in three cups boiling water, and when lukewarm, pass through a blender and strain the juice.

Soak the rice for half an hour. Heat ghee and fry the onion till brown. Drain and set aside. In the same ghee, add the peppercorns, rice and turmeric. Fry for 5 minutes. Add the coconut milk and enough water so that it stands 1" above the rice. Add salt. Bring this to a boil, reduce the heat and cook till the rice is tender. Garnish with the fried onions.

Serves 6

23

Prawn Pullao

½ kg. prawns
1½ cups rice
1 onion (chopped)
6-8 cloves
1 large stick cinnamon
½ tsp. whole peppercorns
4 cardamoms
1 large tomato (chopped)
½ tsp. turmeric
salt to taste

Soak the rice for half an hour at least. Fry the onion till brown, add the cloves, cinnamon, peppercorns, cardamom, rice and tomato. Fry on a slow fire for 5 minutes. Next add the prawns, shelled and de-veined, and mix. Then add the turmeric, salt and 3 cups of water. Bring this to a boil, reduce the heat and cover. Cook till tender and serve hot with green coconut chutney.

Serves 4

24

Jungli Pullao

½ kg. mutton or beef
½ fresh coconut (grated)
4 Kashmiri chillies
½ tsp. cumin
½" piece ginger (chopped)
6-8 flakes garlic (chopped)
½ tsp. khus-khus
6 cloves
1" piece cinnamon
1 tsp. turmeric
½ tsp. ground pepper
1 tsp. ground coriander
2 large onions (chopped)
1½ cups rice
salt and tamarind to taste
a little ghee

Grind together the coconut, chillies, cumin, ginger, garlic, khus-khus, cloves and cinnamon, then add the turmeric, pepper and coriander. Fry one onion lightly and add the ground massala and meat to it. Fry for a few minutes till brown. Just cover with water and cook till tender. Add a little tamarind juice and salt to taste. Cook just a little more and set aside.

Meanwhile soak the rice for at least half an hour. Place the ghee in a pan and fry the other onion and the rice a little. Add the meat and cover with water; this should stand 1″ above the rice. Lower heat and cook on a slow fire still rice is tender. Serve hot.

Serves 4

25

Tomato Pullao

1½ cups rice
1 kg. tomatoes
1 large onion (chopped)
6 cloves
½ tsp. whole peppercorns
1″ piece cinnamon
1 bay leaf
salt to taste

Soak the rice for half an hour. Pass tomatoes through a blender and strain. Fry the onion lightly and add the rice, cloves, peppercorns, cinnamon and bay leaf. Then add the tomato pulp, salt to taste and enough water to stand 1″ above the rice. Lower heat, cover and cook till the rice is done.

Serves 4

26

Prawn Curry

½ kg. prawns (shelled and de-veined)
½ fresh coconut (scraped)
6 Kashmiri chillies
½ tsp. cumin
¼ tsp. peppercorns
1 tblsp. whole coriander
1½ tsp. turmeric
½" piece ginger (chopped)
4 flakes garlic (chopped)
a small ball of tamarind
1 large onion (chopped)
salt to taste
12 whole bhindis (optional)

Grind fine the coconut, chillies, cumin, pepper, coriander, ginger, garlic and tamarind. Add turmeric. Fry the onion till brown. Next add the ground massala and fry well. Add prawns at this stage. Cover with water and cook till done.

You could also add bhindis along with the prawns on the end.

Serves 6

27

Amotik (Sour-hot Curry)

½ kg. prawns, shark or cuttle fish
8 Kashmiri chillies
½ tsp. cumin
½ tsp. peppercorns
¼" piece ginger
2-3 flakes garlic
a small ball of tamarind
vinegar and salt to taste
1 medium onion (sliced)

Grind the chillies, cumin pepper, ginger, garlic and tamarind together, in vinegar. Fry an onion, add the ground massala, fish and salt. Cover with water and cook till the fish is done.

Serves 4

28

Meat Curry

½ kg. mutton or beef
½ fresh coconut (scraped)
6 Kashmiri chillies
½ tsp. cumin
1 tblsp. coriander
1 tblsp. khus-khus
½ tsp. peppercorns
1 tsp. turmeric
½" piece ginger
3 flakes garlic
1 medium onion (chopped)
a few curry leaves
1 tomato (chopped)
tamarind and salt to taste

Toast the coconut, chillies, cumin, coriander and khus-khus in a dry frying pan. Grind all this together with the peppercorns, turmeric, ginger, garlic and tamarind. Fry the onion, add the curry leaves and ground massala and fry well. Next add the tomato and meat. Fry again, add a little water and salt and cook till the meat is tender.

Serves 4

29

Vegetable Curry

½ kg. mixed vegetables (peas, cauliflower, french beans or any seasonal vegetables)
½ fresh coconut (scraped)
1 large bunch each mint and coriander leaves
3 green chillies (chopped)
½" piece ginger
2 flakes garlic
a few peppercorn.
½ tsp. cumin
a small ball of tamarind
1 large onion (chopped)
salt to taste
curry leaves (optional)
1 large tomato (chopped)

Cut the vegetables into small pieces and set aside. Grind together the coconut, coriander and mint leaves, green chillies, ginger, garlic, pepper, cumin and tamarind. Fry the onion in oil or ghee till brown, then fry the vegetables lightly. Add the ground massala, salt and tomato, and the curry leaves. Cover with water and cook till the vegetables are tender.

Serves 4

30

Stick Curry

about $\frac{1}{2}$ kg. meat (cubed very small)
toothpicks
onions, garlic and ginger (as much as desired)
1 onion (sliced)
massala as for meat curry (no. 28)
tamarind and salt to taste
curry leaves

On each toothpick, put a small piece of meat, a piece of onion, another piece of meat, a small piece of fresh ginger, a third piece of meat, and finally a slice of garlic. Continue in this way till all the meat has been used.

Fry the onion, add the massala (as for meat curry) and fry well. Add some curry leaves. Next put in the sticks and cover with water. Cook till the meat is almost tender. Then add the tamarind juice and salt to taste, and cook a little more.

Serves 6

31

Tomato Prawn Curry

1 cup prawns, cleaned and de-veined
20 dry Kashmiri chillies
1 tblsp. coriander
1 tsp. cumin
25 good-sized tomatoes (whole)
½ coconut (scraped)
12 onions (sliced)
6 flakes garlic (chopped)
1" piece ginger (chopped)
5 green chillies
curry leaves
fresh coriander leaves
salt and pepper to taste

Grind the red chillies, coriander, cumin and pepper to a paste and set aside. Steep the tomatoes in hot water and cook for a while. Strain the juice and set aside. Extract juice from the coconut and set this aside, also.

Put some ghee or oil in a pan and fry the sliced onions, garlic and ginger. Add the prawns and salt to this, and fry well. Then add the ground massala, the green chillies, curry and coriander leaves, coconut milk and tomato juice. Cook on a slow fire till it thickens.

Serves 6

32

Drumstick Curry

8 fresh, tender drumsticks
4 dry Kashmiri chillies
½ tsp. cumin
3 cloves
3 heaped tblsp. grated coconut
5 flakes garlic
1 tsp. turmeric
2 small onions (sliced or chopped)
1 tsp. mustard seed
curry leaves

Grind fine the chillies, cumin, cloves, coconut, garlic and turmeric. Skin and cut the drumsticks into small pieces, wash and boil till soft. While boiling, add the ground massala. Season with onion, mustard seeds and curry leaves. Add salt to taste.

Serves 4

33

Meat Ball Curry

about ½ kg mince
1 tsp. turmeric
2 onions (minced)
3 green chillies (minced)
4 flakes garlic (minced)
1" piece ginger (minced)
a bunch each of coriander and mint leaves
1 onion (sliced)
curry leaves
salt and tamarind to taste
massala as for Meat Curry (Recipe 28)

Grind mince fine on a grinding stone or pass through a blender. Mix in the turmeric, minced onions, green chillies, garlic, ginger, coriander and mint leaves. Form into balls. Fry lightly and set aside.

Fry the sliced onion and add the massala (as for Rec. 28). Add the curry leaves and cover with water. When this comes to a boil, add the meat balls and cook. When almost ready, add tamarind juice and salt to taste.

Serves 6

34

Mango Curry

¼ kg. green mangoes (sliced)
6 red chillies
1 dessertspoon coriander
½ tsp. cumin
½ tsp. turmeric
6 flakes garlic
½" piece ginger
2 onions (sliced)
1 tblsp. jaggery
salt to taste

Grind the chillies, coriander, cumin, turmeric, garlic and ginger. Fry the onions till brown, then add the ground massala and fry well. Next add the mangoes and jaggery and cover with water. Add salt to taste. Cook till a little thick.

Serves 4

35

Souraca

1 onion
½ coconut (scraped)
1 tsp. turmeric
1 tsp. cumin
6 cloves garlic
4 red chillies
salt and tamarind juice to taste

Slice the onion and rub each slice with salt. Grind fine the coconut, turmeric, cumin, garlic and chillies. Mix the massala and onion with 4 cups water and boil. When the water is reduced to half, add the tamarind juice and simmer till the curry is thick.

Serves 4

36

Trotters Curry

1 dozen trotters
3 red chillies
1 tsp. turmeric
1 tsp. cumin
1 tblsp. coriander
1" piece ginger
12 flakes garlic
salt and tamarind juice to taste
2 green chillies

Wash trotters well, then dip in boiling water. Scrape hair off with knife. Boil in salt water till tender.

Grind red chillies, turmeric, cumin, coriander, ginger and 8 flakes garlic. Fry the remaining 4 flakes garlic in ghee, add the ground massala and fry again. Put in the trotters along with the water in which they have been cooked and simmer till almost dry. Add tamarind juice and salt to taste. Add the green chillies, slit lengthwise, and simmer till the meat is dropping off the bones.

Serves 6

37

Egg Curry

6 eggs
½ coconut (grated)
4 red chillies
1 tsp. cumin
1 tsp. mustard seeds
4 flakes garlic
¼" piece ginger
1 tsp. turmeric
tamarind juice to taste
1 onion (sliced)
1 tomato (chopped)
salt to taste

Hard-boil the eggs. Shell, cut into halves and set aside. Grind the coconut, chillies, cumin, mustard, garlic and ginger and mix in with the turmeric and tamarind juice. Fry the onion and, when brown, add the massala and tomato. When well fried, add a cup of water and bring it to a boil. Cook for 5 minutes. Lay the eggs gently over the massala, cover the pan and cook for a further 5 minutes. Garnish with coriander leaves.

Serves 6

38

Dal Curry

1½ cups masoor dal
3 tomatoes (chopped)
1 bunch coriander leaves
¼" piece ginger
5 flakes garlic
1 onion (chopped)
¼ tsp. cumin
½ tsp. mustard seeds
curry leaves
salt to taste

Boil the dal and, when cooked, add the chopped tomatoes. Cook till the tomatoes are pulpy. Add the coriander leaves to the dal and set aside. Grind the ginger and garlic. Fry the onion and, when brown, add the cumin and mustard seeds, curry leaves and ginger and garlic paste. When the mustard seeds stop sputtering, pour over the dal and serve.

Serves 6

PORK

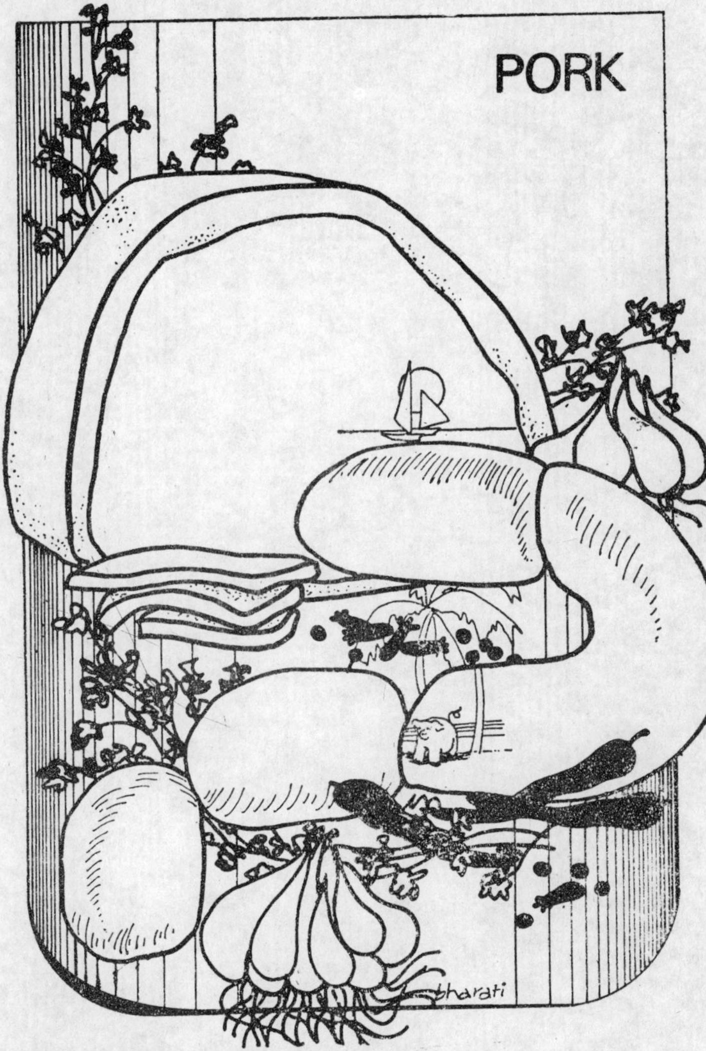

39

Sorpotel (i)

1 kg. pork
¼ kg. liver
2 tsp. chilly powder
1 tsp. ground cumin
1 tsp. ground pepper
1 heaped tsp. ground coriander (to be dry roasted first and then powdered)
1½ tsp. turmeric
3 green chillies
1½ pods garlic
1" piece ginger
vinegar and salt to taste
tamarind to taste

Mix massala powders in a little vinegar to form a paste. Chop fine the green chillies, garlic and ginger and set aside. Boil the pork and liver, cut into pieces, and fry both in their own fat. Add chopped green massala and when fried a little, add the red massala. Fry for 5 minutes, then add the pork-liver water (in which they were boiled) and salt and, when nearly ready, add tamarind juice to taste. Keep for a few days, as sorpotel tastes better as it matures.

Serves 6-8

Sorpotel (ii)

1 kg. pork
¼ kg. liver
2-3 green chillies
2" piece ginger
20 flakes garlic
14 Kashmiri chillies
¾ tsp. peppercorns
¾ tsp. cumin
1½ tsp. coriander (to be dry roasted first)
1" piece turmeric
vinegar, tamarind and salt to taste

Boil the meat with 2 cups water till it reduces to 1 cup. Then cut the meat into small pieces and fry in its own fat. Chop fine the green chillies, ginger and garlic and add to the fried pork. Grind fine the Kashmiri chillies, peppercorns, cumin, coriander and turmeric in vinegar. Add this to the pork and fry well. Then add the cup of water in which the pork was boiled, a little salt, tamarind and vinegar to taste.

Serves 4

40

Grilled Pork Chops

2 kgs. pork chops
8 Kashmiri chillies
4 green chillies
2 tblsp. pepper
1 tblsp. aniseed
1 tsp. ginger
12 cloves garlic
coriander leaves
1 tsp. cumin
3" stick cinnamon
15 cloves
10 cardamoms
1 tblsp. dessicated coconut (optional)
1 tsp. turmeric
salt to taste
1 cup vinegar

Trim chops and beat with a meat mallet. Grind all the massala (i.e., red chillies, green chillies, pepper, aniseed, ginger, garlic, coriander leaves, cumin, cinnamon, cloves, cardamoms, dessicated coconut and turmeric) and mix with the salt and vinegar. Marinate the chops in this massala and keep overnight. Either grill in an oven or over a charcoal fire. Alternatively, put two tablespoons of ghee in a frying pan, put in all the chops, cover and cook till done.

Serves 6

41

Pork Assad

½ kg. pork
1" piece ginger
1 full pod garlic
½ tsp. turmeric
¼ tsp. ground pepper
1" piece cinnamon
5 cloves
2-3 Kashmiri chillies

Prick the pork with a fork and pat salt all over. Grind the ginger and garlic, add turmeric pepper and rub the mixture on the pork.

Warm a little ghee and fry the pork till brown. Then add a little water, the cinnamon, cloves and red chillies (whole) and allow to cook till the water is dry and the pork tender.

Serves 4

42

Fried Pork

½ kg. pork
2-3 green chillies
1" piece ginger
6 flakes garlic
salt to taste
½ tsp. peppercorns
¼ tsp. chilly powder
¼ tsp. turmeric
1 egg
breadcrumbs

Boil the pork and cut into slices. Grind the green chillies, ginger, garlic and peppercorns, and mix in the chilly powder and the turmeric. Add salt. Rub this paste on the boiled pork slices, then dip each slice in the slightly beaten egg and breadcrumbs, and fry.

Serves 6

43

Pork Vindalho

1 kg. pork (cubed)
6 onions
15 flakes garlic
2″ piece ginger
20 Kashmiri chillies
¾ tsp. cumin
½ tsp. peppercorns
1″ piece whole turmeric
6 green chillies (slit)
salt, tamarind, vinegar and sugar
to taste

Finely slice the onions, 6 garlic flakes and 1″ of ginger. Grind together the Kashmiri chillies, cumin, peppercorns, turmeric, and the remaining garlic and ginger. Fry the green massala (i.e., the onions, garlic and ginger) and when brown add the pork, then the ground massala, and fry for 10 minutes. Next add warm water sufficient to cover the pork. When the water has reduced to half, add the green chillies and the sugar, salt, tamarind and vinegar to taste. Simmer on a slow fire till the gravy is thick.

Serves 6-8

44

Pork Roast

3½ kgs. pork
4½ tsps. chilly powder
3 tsps. turmeric
2 tsps. garam massala
2 tsps. coriander
1 tsp. cumin
a little lemon juice
¼ cup salt

Mix the chilly powder, turmeric, garam massala coriander and cumin in lemon juice to form a paste. Prick the Pork and rub in the salt. Spread the paste all over the meat and marinate for 3 hours. Bake at 450° for approximately 5 hours. Baste with ghee every ¾ hours.

Alternatively, fry the pork brown on all sides, then pressure cook with a little water.

Serves 12

CHICKEN AND MEAT

45

Chicken Moelho

1 kg. chicken
2 tsps. cumin
2 tsps. mustard seeds
12 Goa chillies
1 whole pod garlic
½" piece turmeric
1 onion (sliced)
vinegar and salt to taste

Joint the chicken. Grind the cumin, mustard seed, chillies, garlic and turmeric in vinegar. Rub this massala on the chicken joints. Fry the onion till brown and then add the joints. Fry well. Add hot water and cook till tender. Add vinegar and salt to taste when almost ready.

Serves 4

46

Chicken Gizad

1 kg. chicken (beef could be substituted)
2 tsps. cumin
1 tsp. peppercorns
1" piece turmeric
1 onion
5 green chillies
6 flakes garlic
1" piece ginger
vinegar, tamarind and salt to taste
1 wineglass coconut milk

Cut the chicken, salt and set aside. Grind the cumin, pepper and turmeric (alternatively, powders could be used), then slice the onion, green chillies garlic and ginger.

Fry the sliced onion till brown. Add the ginger garlic and green chillies followed by the ground massala and chicken. Cover the pan and when the water has evaporated, fry nicely. Then add boiling water (to cover the chicken) a little vinegar and tamarind and cook for 5 minutes. When almost ready, add the coconut milk.

Serves 4-6

47

Chicken Baffad

1 kg. chicken (jointed)
8 Kashmiri chillies
1" piece turmeric
20 peppercorns
½ tsp. cumin
5 cloves
1" piece cinnamon
2 onions
3 green chillies
1" piece ginger
12 flakes garlic
1 coconut
vinegar and salt to taste

Grind together the Kashmiri chillies, turmeric, pepper, cumin, cloves and cinnamon. Finely chop the onions, green chillies, ginger and garlic. Scrape the coconut, add a cupful of hot water, cool, then pass through a blender. Strain the thick juice. Repeat process and strain their milk. Set aside. Salt the chicken. Fry the onions, add the chicken and the green chopped massala. Next add the ground massala and fry well. Add the thick and thin coconut milk (this juice should just cover the chicken) and cook. When nearly done, add vinegar and cook a little more till chicken is tender.

Serves 6

48

Chicken Shakuti

1 kg. chicken (or mutton)
3 tsps. coriander
8 Kashmiri chillies
½ tsp. cumin
1 tsp. fenugreek seeds
5 peppercorns
2 tsps. peanuts
½ coconut (scraped)
1" piece turmeric
4 cardamoms
6 cloves
1" piece cinnamon
1 sour lemon
salt to taste

Roast the coriander, chillies, cumin, fenugreek, pepper, peanuts and coconut on a dry pan. Add the turmeric, cardamoms, cloves and cinnamon and grind all finely.

Warm some ghee and brown the ground massala well. Add chicken pieces, salt and mix well. When cooked, add the juice of one lemon.

Serves 6

49

Assada

1½ kg. beef or mutton
4 green chillies
1" piece ginger
1 pod garlic
2 tsps. turmeric
¼ tsp. pepper
3 onions (sliced)
vinegar and salt to taste
2 whole red chillies (broken up)

Grind the chillies, ginger and garlic and add the turmeric and pepper powders. Mix them all with vinegar to form a paste. Prick the meat with a fork and rub in the mixture. Marinate for 3 hours. Brown the sliced onions and add the meat. Brown evenly on all sides. Add the broken red chillies, a little warm water, cover and cook till tender.

Serves 6

50

Bifes

½ kg. meat (cubed)
1" piece ginger
12 flakes garlic
4 green chillies
3 onions (sliced)
1 tsp. turmeric
¼ tsp. ground pepper
1 tsp. sugar
2 tblsp. vinegar
salt to taste

Crush the ginger, garlic and green chillies. Brown the onions, add the meat and brown till the water dries. Put in the powdered massala and sugar, and the crushed ginger, garlic and chillies and brown well. Cover with warm water and cook till the meat is tender. Add the vinegar and salt and cook a little more.

Serves 6

51

Mince

½ kg. mince
½ kg. onions
2" piece ginger (chopped)
12 flakes garlic (chopped)
3-4 green chillies (chopped)
1 tsp. turmeric
¼ tsp. chilly powder
½ tsp. ground cumin
½ tsp. ground pepper
1 tomato (chopped)
a bunch each, mint and coriander leaves
a little water

Fry half the onions in ghee till brown, then add the ginger, garlic and green chillies. Next, put in the mince with the turmeric, chilly, cumin and pepper powders and mix well. Add the tomato and the chopped mint and coriander. Add salt to taste, water and cook till dry. Add remaining onions and cook till mince is dry.

Serves 6-8

52

Potato Mince Cutltes

1 kg. potatoes
½ tsp. pepper
salt to taste
1 egg (slightly beaten)
breadcrumbs
mince (recipe 51)

Boil the potatoes. Mash and add salt and pepper. Take a portion the size of an orange, hollow out a little and put in some mince. Form into cutlets, dip into egg and breadcrumbs and fry.

Serves 6

53

Fried Brain

½ kg. brain
green chutney (recipe 78)
1 egg—slightly beaten
breadcrumbs
salt and pepper to taste

Parboil the brain with a little salt. Slice. Spread the chutney on either side of the brain, dip in the egg, then breadcrumbs, and fry.

Serves 6

54

Chilly Fry

½ kg. meat (cubed)
8 large onions
8 peppercorns
2" piece ginger
6 flakes garlic
a bunch each, coriander and mint leaves
4-6 green chillies
salt and pepper to taste
a little tamarind

Boil the meat with one onion, peppercorns and salt. Slice the remaining onions, and chop fine the ginger, garlic, coriander and mint leaves, and green chillies. Fry the remaining onions till they are transparent. Add the chopped green massala, then the meat and seasoning. Next pour in the water in which the meat was boiled and when the meat is nearly done, add the tamarind. Cook till dry.

Serves 6

55

Salt Meat

1½ kg. meat
1½ dessertspoon salt
1 dessertspoon saltpetre
½ cup vinegar
½ cup lemon juice

Prick the meat well and rub in the salt. Roast the saltpetre and grind. Add this to the vinegar and lemon juice and pour over the meat. Put the meat in an earthenware crock, cover and keep under a weight. Prick and turn the meat twice a day for 7 days. Boil with enough water to just cover the meat. Cook till tender. (This should only be made in the winter otherwise the meat is likely to spoil.)

Serves 8

56

Salt Tongue

1 tongue
2 tblsp. salt
2 dessertspoons saltpetre
2 tsp. papadkhar
½ cup vinegar
½ cup lemon juice
2 heaped tblsp. jaggery

Make a mixture of the salt, saltpetre and papadkhar. Prick the tongue and rub this mixture on it. Heat the vinegar and the lemon juice and dissolve the jaggery in it. Pour over the tongue and keep in the refrigerator in an earthenware crock for 5 days turning it as often as possible. Boil it with its liquor, add water if necessary and cook till tender.

Serves 4

57

Massala Liver

½ kg. liver
4 flakes garlic
1" piece ginger
1" piece cinnamon
5 green chillies
6 peppercorns
¼ tsp. cumin
vinegar, salt and sugar to taste
4 onions (chopped)
2 tomatoes (chopped)

Boil the liver with the garlic, ginger and cinnamon. Next grind the green chillies, peppercorns and cumin. Mix this massala with sugar, salt and a little vinegar. Slice the liver and spread the massala over the slices. Set aside for half an hour. Fry the onions till they are brown, add the liver and its water (in which it was boiled) and the chopped tomatoes. Cook till dry.

Serves 6

58

Pan Rolls

1 cup flour
2 large eggs
milk (enough for a thin batter)
mince (recipe 51)
breadcrumbs
salt to taste

Sieve the flour. Make a hole in the centre and put in one egg and enough milk to form into a thin batter. Beat with a wooden spoon till smooth. Set aside for about 15 minutes. Heat a frying pan with a few drops of oil and pour in a spoonful of batter. Spread evenly and remove from fire after cooking for 2 minutes. Put some mince into it, and roll. Coat with the other slightly beaten egg, dip in breadcrumbs and fry in a shallow pan till light brown.

Serves 6

59

Patties

1 cup flour
½ cup cornflour
1 tblsp. ghee
a little water
mince (recipe 51)

Make a dough of the flour, ¼ cup cornflour, ½ tblsp. ghee and water. Knead into a smooth dough. Roll the dough out into a chappati. Make a paste of the other ¼ cup cornflour and ½ tblsp. ghee and spread over the chappati. Sprinkle a little flour over this and roll the chappati tight. Cut into small pieces. Roll out each piece, put in a little mince, seal with a little water on the outer edges of the pastry and deep fry.

Serves 8

60

Beef Olives

½ kg. steak meat
1" piece ginger
10 peppercorns
1 bunch mint leaves
1½" piece cinnamon
1 green chilly
a slice of bread (soaked and drained)
1-2 rashers bacon
2 large onions (minced)
2 tsps. flour
salt to taste

Beat each piece of meat with a meat chopper and set aside. Grind together the ginger, peppercorns, mint, cinnamon and the green chilly. Cut the bacon fine and mix in with this massala. Squeeze the slice of bread and add to the massala with one minced onion. Lay a teaspoon of this stuffing on each slice of meat, roll into a sausage and secure with a piece of string. Then fry in a little ghee till brown. Remove. In the same ghee brown the other minced onion, add the flour and a cup of water to form a gravy. Add salt to taste. Finally add the meat and stew gently till done. Remove the string and serve warm.

Serves 6

61

Massala Fry

½ kg. mutton or beef undercut
6 red chillies
1 tblsp. turmeric
1 tsp. cumin
6 flakes garlic
salt to taste
1 tsp. pepper
1 tsp. ginger
4 cloves
2 sticks cinnamon
3 cardamoms
tamarind juice to taste

Cube the meat and beat in order to tenderize. Grind all the massalas with the tamarind juice and roll the meat in the same. Marinate for 2 hours. Heat oil in a frying pan and fry the meat. Cover the pan and put a weight on the lid so that the meat is pressed down well. Simmer for 20 minutes, then add one cup warm water and cook till the meat is tender.

Serves 6

62

Brain Cutlets

1 brain (cow's or 2 sheep's)
1 onion (minced)
2 green chillies (minced)
a bunch each, coriander and mint leaves
4 flakes garlic (minced)
2 slices bread (soaked in milk)
2 eggs
salt to taste

Boil the brain in salted, boiling water for 10 minutes. Lift out and wash. Mix with minced onion, chillies, mint and coriander leaves, garlic, bread (drained) eggs and salt. Then form into cutlets and fry.

Serves 6

63

Steak

1 kg. undercut
2 green chillies
1 pod garlic
1" piece ginger
salt to taste
½ tsp. peppercorns
2 tblsp. vinegar
2 tblsp. soy sauce
2 tblsp. oil
onions, potatoes, tomatoes and capsicum for garnishing

Trim the meat and beat to tenderize. Grind the chillies, garlic, ginger and peppercorns and mix in with the vinegar, soy sauce and oil. Mix meat in this mixture and marinate for 3-4 hours. Heat a little oil in a frying pan and fry onions (cut in rings) for 3-4 minutes. Drain and set aside. Fry the potatoes as french fries and set aside. Fry the tomatoes and capsicums, cut in quarters, and set aside. Now fry the steaks, one at a time, on a very high flame. Turn and fry the other side. When all the meat has cooked, mix the remaining marinade with a little water and pour into the frying pan. Cook for 5 minutes. If desired, mix in a little cornflour to thicken the gravy. (The cornflour should be mixed with a little cold water to form a paste before adding to the gravy.) When all the steaks are done arrange on a platter and garnish with onions, potatoes, tomatoes and capsicum.

Serves 6

64

Mince Cutlets

½ kg. mince (beef or mutton)
3 onions
4-5 green chillies
1" piece ginger
8 flakes garlic
one bunch coriander leaves
1 tsp. pepper
1 egg
3 slices bread (soaked in milk and drained)
salt and vinegar to taste

Mince the onions, green chillies, ginger, garlic and coriander. Add these to the minced meat, along with the seasoning, egg and bread (drained). Add a dash of vinegar. From into cutlets and fry.

Serves 6-8

65

Beef Loaf

½ kg. minced beef
4 rashers bacon
3 green chillies
2 slices bread (soaked and drained)
2 eggs
salt, pepper and nutmeg to taste

Mince the bacon and green chillies. Add the bread, eggs, beef and seasoning. Tie in waxed paper or cloth and steam in a vessel of boiling water for an hour.

Serves 6

66

Kidneys and Tomatoes

3 sheep's kidneys
2 rashers bacon
6 large ripe tomatoes
a bunch each, mint and coriander leaves
6 flakes garlic
½" piece ginger
2-3 green chillies
1 large onion (minced)
salt and pepper to taste

Wash kidneys, clean and cut into small pieces. Chop fine the bacon, tomatoes, coriander and mint leaves, garlic, ginger, chillies and onion. Fry massalas in a little oil, add kidneys, salt and pepper, and cook till done. Serve on fried toast.

Serves 6

67

Baffad

½ kg. meat (cubed)
¼ kg. mixed vegetable
½ tsp. cumin
4 Kashmiri chillies
1 tsp. coriander
½ tsp. ground pepper
8 flakes garlic
1" piece ginger
1 tsp. turmeric
1 onion
2 green chillies
salt and vinegar to taste

Boil the meat with the vegetables and set aside. Grind the cumin, chillies, coriander, pepper, 4 garlic flakes and half the ginger. Add turmeric. Chop fine the onion, the remaining flakes garlic and ginger, and the green chillies. Brown the onion in oil, add the chopped massala, and then the ground massala. Next, put in the meat and vegetables. Add salt and vinegar to taste and cook on a slow fire till the meat is dry.

Serves 6

68

Baffad of Sheep's Tongue

3 tongues
4 Goa chillies
½" piece turmeric
1 tsp. cumin
1" piece cinnamon
½ tsp. pepper
4 flakes garlic
½" piece ginger
1 green chilly
3 cloves
1 onion
tamarind, salt and
vinegar to taste

Boil the tongues, cut into pieces and set aside. Grind fine the chillies, turmeric, cumin, cinnamon, pepper, garlic, ginger, green chilly and cloves. Brown the sliced onion in ghee. Fry the massala and then add the sliced tongues. Add the tamarind water and the water in which the tongues were boiled, vinegar and salt to taste, and simmer till the gravy is thick.

Serves 6

PICKLES AND CHUTNEYS

69

Lime Pickle

30 sour limes
4 tblsp. dry Kashmiri chillies
2 tblsp. turmeric
2 tblsp. cumin
a handful curry leaves
2½ cups vinegar
2 tblsp. mustard seeds
4 pods garlic
6" piece ginger
10 green chillies
4 tblsp. sugar
2 tblsp. salt
2½ cups oil

Cut the limes into quarters, salt and keep for 3-4 days. Powder the chillies, turmeric, cumin and mustard. Keep the garlic whole, and the ginger, sliced. Put the oil on the fire and when hot, add the garlic and curry leaves. When the garlic is browned, add the dry massala and green chillies. Then pour in all the vinegar and throw in the limes after washing them in vinegar. Add the sugar and cook for 15 minutes. Cool and bottle.

70

Mustard Mango Pickle—Miscut

50 mangoes (medium sized)
salt
4 cups chilly powder
2 cups turmeric
2 cups fenugreek (pounded)
4 tblsp. mustard seed (pounded)
½ tsp. asafoetida
one cup oil

Cut the mangoes in four almost all the way down. Stuff with salt and let them stand for 5 days under pressure. Turn mangoes every day. On the fifth day, wash them in brine and stuff with the following:

Warm a cup of oil and fry the chilly, turmeric, fenugreek, mustard and asafoetida for 5 minutes. Then stuff the mangoes with this mixture. Place in a jar and cover the mangoes with hot oil.

71

Kassaundi

3½ kgs. mangoes or brinjals (peeled and sliced fine)
1¾ cups chilly powder
4 heaped tblsp. turmeric
4 heaped tblsp. mustard seeds
1¾ cups salt
4 cups sugar
5½ cups oil
4 heaped tblsp. cumin
4 heaped tblsp. fenugreek
10" piece ginger
13 small pods garlic
1¾ cups tamarind (soaked in vinegar and strained)
5½ cups vinegar
a handful of curry leaves

Soak mangoes in salt for 12 hours. Tie in a clean cloth and squeeze out the water. Heat oil, add curry leaves and all the massalas, previously pounded. Then add a little vinegar. Put in the mangoes and mix well. Add the remaining vinegar, tamarind, sugar and sufficient oil to cover. Bottle.

72

Mixed Vegetable Pickle

1 kg. mixed vegetable
1 cup sugar
a handful curry leaves
4 tsps. cumin
1½" piece turmeric
4 tsps. mustard seed
20 red Kashmiri chillies
2 whole pods garlic
2 tsp. fenugreek
2 cups oil
salt and vinegar to taste

Clean vegetables and cut into pieces. Sprinkle with salt and dry in the sun for a day. Drain out the water. Grind cumin, turmeric, mustard, chillies, garlic, and fenugreek in vinegar. Heat the oil. Put in the curry leaves and the ground massala and fry well. Add the sugar, a little more vinegar and the vegetables. Cook on a slow fire for about 20 minutes. Cool and bottle.

73

Mango Chutney

$1\frac{3}{4}$ kgs. mangoes (chopped)
4 cups sugar
$2\frac{1}{2}$ cups vinegar
5″ piece ginger
7 pods garlic
4 tblsp. chilly powder
2 tblsp. mustard seed
4 tblsp. salt
2 cups raisins

Boil the fruit with the sugar and vinegar. Grind the ginger and garlic in a little vinegar, and add the chilly powder, mustard, salt and raisins. Cook all this with the mangoes till they are soft. Bottle when cool.

74

Green Chilly Pickle

900 gms. green chillies
2 tblsp. cumin
one handful amchur
1" piece turmeric
3 pods garlic (sliced)
2 cups oil
vinegar, sugar, salt to taste

Pound cumin, amchur, turmeric and salt together. Mix in with the green chillies. Heat the oil and throw in the sliced garlic. When this is brown, put in the chilly mixture, add vinegar and sugar to taste and cook well. Cool and bottle.

75

Lime Pickle

30 limes
the juice of another 30 limes
4 tblsp. chilly powder
2 tblsp. turmeric
salt

Cut the limes in four, fill with salt and keep in the sun for 4-5 days till soft. Then make a paste of the chilly and turmeric powders with the lemon juice and fill into the limes. Pour the rest of the juice in the jar with the limes. Keep in the sun for another week till pickled. This pickle should be eaten quickly as it does not keep too long.

76

Tendli Pickle

200 tendlis
4 cups oil
20 green chillies (minced)
7 pods garlic (minced)
6" piece ginger (minced)
2 cups vinegar
4 tblsp. chilly powder
2 tblsp. turmeric
4 tblsp. sugar

Cut tendlis into quarters, add salt and hang to let the water drain, overnight. Boil the oil, and add the green chillies, garlic and ginger. When well fried, add the vinegar, chilly powder, turmeric, tendlis and sugar. Bring to one fast boil and then remove from fire. Bottle, making sure the pickle is covered with oil.

77

Dry Bombay Duck Pickle

12 large Bombay ducks
1 pod garlic
2" piece ginger
1 tsp. cumin
1 tblsp. turmeric
1" piece cinnamon
3 cloves
½ cup vinegar
½ cup oil
salt to taste

Clean the Bombay ducks and cut into pieces. Fry and set aside. Grind the garlic, ginger, cumin, turmeric, cinnamon and cloves in vinegar and brown in the oil. Add the Bombay ducks, cook, cool briefly, and bottle.

78

Green Chutney

½ coconut (scraped)
1 large bunch coriander leaves
2 green chillies
sugar and salt to taste
½″ piece ginger
2-3 flakes garlic
4 peppercorns
tamarind (size of a walnut)

Grind all the ingredients to a fine paste, adding sugar and salt to taste. Eat fresh, as it does not keep for long.

SWEETS

79

Baath

½ kg. semolina
2 coconuts
6 eggs
4 cups sugar
8 tblsp. butter
½ tsp. salt
½ tsp. baking powder
rose water to taste

Scrape coconuts, avoiding the brown husk, and grind in rose water to form a fine paste. Beat eggs, sugar and butter till fluffy. Add the semolina and mix well. Blend in the coconut paste and add salt and baking powder. Set aside for 12 hours or overnight, to rise. If the dough is a little stiff, add a little milk to soften. Grease some thalis and pour in the mixture. Bake in a moderate oven till done.

Serves 8

80

Semolina Balls

2 cups semolina
1 cup sugar
½ cup water
1 tblsp. ghee
½ coconut (scraped)
rose water to taste
a few cardamoms, raisins and nuts

Make a syrup of the sugar and water. Fry semolina lightly in ghee and when syrup is sticky, add semolina, scraped coconut, rose water and cardamoms (crushed). Lastly, add nuts and raisins. Stir till thick. Cool a bit and form into balls, and serve.

Serves 8

81

Kulkuls

1-2 coconuts
1½ cups semolina
4 cups flour
4 eggs (yolks only)
a little butter

Scrape the coconuts and extract the milk. Mix in the semolina, flour, egg yolks and butter and add the coconut milk to form a stiff dough. Knead well, adding butter as you knead to form a soft dough. Keep covered for 15 minutes. Then taking small balls of the dough, shape over a comb or a fork to form curls. Fry in hot oil till light brown. (These kulkuls can be sugar-coated by dipping them in a thick sugar syrup.)

Serves 12

82

Rose De Coque or Waffles

3 eggs
4 heaped tblsp. flour
2 tblsp. sugar
1 cup milk or coconut milk

Beat the eggs well and mix in nicely with the flour. Add the sugar and milk and mix well. Heat half a bottle of oil in a deep pan. Dip the mould in the oil and then into the mixture, place it in the oil again and fry till light brown. Remove waffle from the mould and continue till all the batter is used.

Serves 6

83

Bolo De Portugal

½ kg. almonds (cashewnuts may be substituted, using almond essence)
4 cups semolina
4 cups sugar (ground)
2 cups butter
16 eggs
one wineglass brandy
rose water

Grind the almonds fine in rose water to form a paste. Add semolina and mix in the sugar and butter and beat till it turns white, then add the yolks of eight eggs, one at a time, the ground almonds, brandy and lastly the stiffly beaten egg whites of 16 eggs. Bake in a moderate oven till done.

Serves 12

84

Coconut Drops

½ cup sugar
1 coconut (scraped and ground)
a few almonds and raisins
3 eggs
rose water to taste
a little flour

Make a thick syrup of the sugar and a little water. Add the coconut and cook till it thickens. Remove from the fire and cool. Add almonds and raisins, 1 whole egg and the yolks of the other 2 eggs. Add rose water to taste and mix in a little flour so that the batter is slightly stiff. Form the mixture into little balls and dip the bottoms into the whites of the 2 eggs. Place them on thalis which have been previously greased and floured. Bake in a moderate oven till done.

Serves 8

85

Ribbon Cake

10 eggs
2 cups sugar
4 cups rice flour
2 cups butter
3 different colcurs and essences

Mix the yolks of the eggs with the sugar first, then add the flour and butter gradually. When the whole is well mixed, divide the batter into 3 parts, colouring differently, as desired and with the desired essences. Pour one part into a greased pan, followed by the other two—first the white layer, then the pink, and finally the green. Bake in a moderate oven till done.

Serves 8

86

Bibinca

3¾ cups sugar
½ cup water
a few cardamoms (crushed)
10 eggs (yolks only)
2 cups coconut milk (thick)
1 cup flour
¾ cup melted ghee

Make a thin syrup of the sugar, water and cardamoms. Cool and strain. Beat egg yolks and add the coconut milk, flour and the cooled syrup. Keep standing for an hour before baking. After an hour, put in a tablespoon or more of ghee in a pan. Place over the fire, and when hot, pour a little batter to form a layer. Cook till brown. Then pour another tablespoon of ghee over this layer and put it under a grill. When it is hot, add another layer of batter. Cook till brown and continue layering until all the batter has been used. Cool and keep overnight before cutting into slices.

Serves 12

87

Potato Bibinca

½ kg. potatoes
6 eggs
1½ cups sugar
4 heaped tblsp. flour
2 heaped tblsp. semolina
milk of 2 large coconuts (only thick milk)
6 level tblsp. butter
12 cardamoms (powdered)

Boil the potatoes, mash and set aside. Make a syrup of the sugar and cool. Mix the flour and semolina with a little coconut milk and blend in the yolks of the eggs, one at a time, beating lightly after each addition. Add the boiled, mashed potatoes and the rest of the coconut milk. Then add the whites of the eggs (well beaten). Heat the ghee in a pan, pour in the batter and bake. If preferred, bake in layers, as in the previous recipe.

Serves 8-10

88

Nankatais

4 cups flour
$1\frac{1}{2}$ cups ghee
$1\frac{3}{4}$ cups sugar (ground fine)
a dash of salt
1 tsp. baking powder
1 tsp. icecream essence
1 tsp. orange or
rasberry essence

Soften the ghee with the palm of your hand for some time. Then add to it, sugar, salt, flour and baking powder. Mix well. Form into small balls, place on a greased baking sheet and bake in a slow oven. (Let the batter stand for an hour before baking.)

Serves 12-14

89

Neuris

Pastry :

1 cup ghee
$\frac{1}{2}$ kg. flour
a pinch of salt
water for dough

Filling :

$\frac{1}{2}$ kg. semolina
$\frac{1}{2}$ kg. sugar
$\frac{1}{2}$ tblsp. blanched almonds
1$\frac{1}{2}$ tblsp. pistachio or chironji nuts
cornflour for sprinkling
3 tblsp. raisins
1 coconut (grated)
ghee as required
cardamom powder
ghee for frying and for applying between layers of dough

For the pastry, mix the ghee and flour till the mixture looks like fine breadcrumbs. Dissolve the salt in water and mix with the flour and ghee to make a pliable dough. Cover and keep in a cool place.

For the filling, heat ghee in a pan, and when it boils, put in the semolina and fry well, stirring from time to time so that it is evenly and lightly browned. Add sugar and fry a little while longer. Or, make a syrup with the sugar and water and add this to the semolina. Stir continuously, on low heat, till the mixture dries. Add the grated coconut. Before removing from the fire, add the dried fruit which has been previously fried. Mix well and cool.

To make the neuris, divide the pastry dough into small balls, and roll out into small chappatis. Apply ghee and a sprinkling of cornflour over each and sandwich about 7 together. The last one should be "clean". Roll out so that the layers adhere to one another. Cut out rounds. Put a spoonful of the semolina filling in each, wet edges and press down firmly to form crescents. Trim edges with a pastry cutter. Deep fry till light brown.

Serves 12

90

Coconut Pancakes

½ kg. flour
6 eggs
a pinch of salt
1 cup milk
ghee for frying

Filling: *2 scraped coconuts*
sugar to taste
juice of 1-2 lemons
a few raisins

Sift the flour, and make a hole in the centre. Add salt and the beaten eggs. Mix gradually with your hands, stirring a little of the flour from the sides till it has all mixed with the egg. Add the milk, stirring till the batter is of pouring consistency. Let it stand for a few minutes.

Filling: Mix all the ingredients together.

Place a frying pan on the fire. When hot,.rub with a little melted ghee, pour a spoonful of batter in, and spread it round the pan evenly. Cook for a little while, tip pan over and fill pancake with the coconut filling.

Serves 8

91

Coconut Toffee

2 cups granulated sugar
1 cup milk
4 tblsp. butter
2 cups freshly grated coconut
2 tblsp. cashewnuts (chopped)
rose or almond essence

Put the sugar, milk, 2 tblsp. butter and coconut in a pan, place it on a slow fire and stir till every grain of sugar has dissolved. Cook to soft ball stage (when a little dropped in cold water forms a soft ball). Add the other 2 tblsp. butter and take the pan off the fire. Beat for a while, then add essence. Pour into buttered thalis and when cool, cut into squares.

Makes 2 trays

92

Banana Fritters

4 large bananas
2 eggs
sugar to taste
4 tblsp. flour
a little milk
a dash of salt

Mash bananas. Beat eggs with sugar and mix in the bananas, flour and enough milk to form a thick batter. Heat ghee in a frying pan and ladle in spoonfuls of batter. Brown on both sides and drain. Sprinkle sugar over the fritters and serve.

Serves 6

93

Doughnuts

Dough for doughnuts should be as soft as [can be handled, A soft dough is easier to roll when well chilled. Cut doughnuts with a floured cutter and allow to stand for 15 minutes. Deep fry in hot fat. Do not fry too many at a time as fat will cool rapidly. Turn only once when frying.

2 tblsp. shortening
¾ cup sugar
2 well-beaten eggs
¾ cup milk
3½ cups flour
1 tsp. salt
5 tsps. baking powder
1 tsp. cinnamon
1 tsp. nutmeg

Cream shortening and sugar; add eggs and beat well. Add the milk then the flour sifted with salt, baking powder and spices. Allow to stand for 15 minutes. Deep fry in hot fat. Drain.

Makes 3 dozen

94

Almond Puffs

4 tblsp. semolina
sugar, equalling the weight of the almonds and coconuts
2 coconuts (grated)
4 eggs (yolks only)
3½ tblsp. almonds or cashews (grated)
2 tsps. vanilla essence

Make a syrup of the sugar. When it thickens, add the coconut and cook for 5 minutes. Remove from fire and cool. Beat the yolks, add the semolina and almonds and add this to the syrup. Let the mixture stand for 3 hours. Lastly, add vanilla. Form into little cakes and bake in a moderate oven.

Serves 12

95

Rickjaw

3 bottles milk
juice of one lemon
4 tblsp. almonds (or cashews, with almond essence)
1 wineglass rose water
1 egg white
1½ cups sugar

Boil the milk and while boiling, add the juice of the lemon. When the milk has split, strain through a muslin bag till all the when has drained out. Then, grind the paneer with the almonds and rose water till fine. Beat the egg white, mix it in with this paste, add sugar and cook on a slow fire to soft ball stage. Place on greased pans and cut into squares.

Makes 2 trays

96

Cordeal

4 cups almonds (or cashews)
$3\frac{3}{4}$ cups sugar
rose water
one tumbler-full water
cochineal

Grind the almonds in rose water, and make a syrup of the sugar and water. Colour the syrup with a few drops of cochineal. When the syrup thickens, add the almonds. Stir to soft ball stage, then pour onto greased pans and cut into squares.

Makes 2 trays

97

Cashewnut Toffee

4 cups cashews (ground)
2 bottles milk
2 cups sugar
8 tblsp. butter
vanilla and almond essence
colouring

Grate nuts, add to milk and sugar and cook on a slow fire. When thick, add the butter. Cook to soft ball stage, add essences and colouring and pour onto buttered pans. Cool and cut into squares.

Makes 3 trays

98

Marzipan

4 cups almonds (or cashews)
4 cups sugar
whites of 3 eggs (2 if large)
rose water
almond essence (if using cashews)
colouring

Soak the almonds in water the previous evening. Remove skins and grind fine in rose water. (If using cashews, grate and mix with rose water and almond essence.) Put the almond paste, sugar and egg whites on a slow fire and cook to soft ball stage. Pour onto a marble slab when a little cool and knead till soft. (You may need a little icing sugar if the mixture is sticky.) Flavour and colour and either shape into fruit or put into a rubber mould.

Makes about 200 pieces

99

Mock Marzipan

soft pith of 1 kg. 800 gms. pumpkin
4 coconuts (scraped)
4 cups almonds or cashews with almond essence
6 cups sugar
8 tblsp. butter
3 eggs (whites only)
essences and colouring
rose water

Scrape out the pith of the pumpkin and grind. Grind fine the almonds and coconuts in rose water. Place the pumpkin and the sugar on the fire and cook until the former is well cooked. Mix in the whites of the eggs, well beaten. Add the almonds and ground coconut and a wineglass of rose water. Stir constantly on a slow fire. Cook to soft ball stage, then add the butter. When it reaches the right consistency (i. e., when a little taken in the palm of your hand can be moulded) remove from fire. Stir for five minutes and form into fruit.

Marzipan Fruit
Strawberries: Strawberry essence, cochineal. Form into

strawberries, roll in granulated sugar and stick a leaf made of crepe paper on top of the fruit.

Oranges and Peaches:	Orange essence, orange or yellow colouring. Shape into fruit and stick a leaf at the top.

Makes about 150 pieces

100

Seed Cake

6 eggs
½kg. sugar
½ kg. semolina
½ kg. butter
1 tblsp. caraway seeds
1 tsp. vanilla essence

Mix the yolks of the eggs with the sugar and add the semolina and butter. Add caraway seeds, stirring continuously. Leave overnight. Then add vanilla essence and bake in a moderate oven till done.

Serves 8

Glossary

Condiments

almonds	badam
aniseed	saunf
arrowroot	araroht
asafoetida	hing
baking powder	pakane ka soda
bay leaf (or Cassia)	tej patta
black pepper or peppercorns	kali mirch
basil	gulal tulsi
breadcrumbs	sukhi double roti ka chora
caraway seeds	shah jeera
cardamom	elaichi
cinnamon	dalchini
cashewnuts	kaju
cloves	laung
cochineal	gulabi rang
coconut	narial
cariander leaves	hara dhaniya
coriander seeds	sukha dhaniya
cumin	jeera
curry leaves	meethi neem ke patte
dry coconut	khopra
dry ginger	sonth
fenugreek	methi

fennel	hasha
ginger	adrak
garlic	lassan
green chillies	hari mirch
groundnuts	moongphali
jack fruit seeds	kathal ke beej
jaggery	gur
lemon rind	nimbu ka chilka
mace	javitri
marjoram	ban tulsi
mango powder	amchur
mint leaves	pudina
nutmeg	jaiphal
onion seeds	pyaz ke beej
parsley	ajmooda ka patta
pistachio	pista
poppy seeds	khus-khus
raisins	kishmish
red chillies	lal mirch
saffron	kesar
sage	seesti
sesame seed	til
sugar candy	misri
tamarind	imli
turmeric	haldi
tymol seeds	ajwain
thyme	hasha
vinegar	sirka

Vegetables

beetroot	chukander
bitter gourd	karela
brinjal	baingan
beans	sem
cabbage	bandh gobi
capsicum	bari mirch
carrot	gajar
cauliflower	phool gobi
celery	ajwain ka patta
cucumber	kakri
colocasia leaf	arvi ka patta
drumstick	saijan ki phali
dry beans	chauli or ravaan
elephant yam	zimikand
fenugreek leaves	methi
french beans	pharas bean
fresh mint	hara pudina
green peas	mattar
ladies finger	bhindi
mushrooms	kukar moote or guchi
onions	pyaz
potatoes	aloo
pumpkin	kaddu
radish	mooli
ridge gourd	torai
snake gourd	chirchira
spinach	palak
spring onion	hara pyaz
sprouted beans	phuli hari chauli

sweet potato	shakarkand
turnip	shalgam
tomato	tamatar
white gourd	lauki
yam	suren

Lentils and Cereals

barley	juwar
bengal gram	chana dal
black gram	urad dal (or maash)
corn	makkai
flour	maida
green gram	moong dal
gram flour	besan
large white gram	kabuli chana
millet flour	bajra atta
red gram	arhar dal
sago	sagodana
semolina	suji
vermicelli	sevain

(This is a comprehensive glossary, and some of the items listed may not be part of the recipes in this book.)